# Dancing with the Angels

Other Books by the Author:

OWL WOMAN—"A Shaman's Story"

UP THE TREE—"A Shaman's Adventure between the Worlds"

THE SHAMAN'S GRANDDAUGHTER

WALKABOUT WITH THE ELK RUNNER—"A Love Story"

THE BEEKEEPER—"A Story that transcends Time"

ONE MAGICAL JOURNEY—"And what it Taught Me"

DANCING WITH THE ANGELS is Owl Woman's 7<sup>th</sup> book.

# Dancing with the Angels

## *My Search for the Sacred*

## Owl Woman

iUniverse, Inc.
Bloomington

# Dancing with the Angels
## My Search for the Sacred

iUniverse books may be ordered through booksellers or by contacting:

iUniverse
1663 Liberty Drive
Bloomington, IN 47403
www.iuniverse.com
1-800-Authors (1-800-288-4677)

ISBN: 978-1-4759-6485-1 (sc)
ISBN: 978-1-4759-6486-8 (ebk)

Library of Congress Control Number: 2012922733

Printed in the United States of America

iUniverse rev. date: 12/04/2012

# CONTENTS

This book is dedicated to all those who feel somehow out of step, different, more sensitive or perhaps more aware than the rest. Those who see faeries and dream of "Dancing with the Angels". May you always have the courage to march to a different drummer.

A huge thank you to my daughter Sondra and my husband Frank for their able assistance with this book.

# INTRODUCTION

"Angels at my Bedside"


They float in on the near darkness
and pale blue moon shine

They come when you most need them
but least expect them

Their touch is only the weight of a feather
but it changes everything


Their beings are luminous
like the soft glow of a burning out candle


Their numbers are legion

They have been on duty since the dawn of time
and they shall stay after the end of days

They are the Elohim, the divine Feminine

They watch over the cribs of Infants

They visit us

# CHAPTER ONE

## "The Kinfolk"

What school child hasn't stared up into the star-filled sky and wondered to himself, "Is this where I came from?" Or what kid hasn't asked his parents "Mom, Dad, who did I come from?" Meaning, of course, who were my people? Where did they come from, those ancestors of long ago? If you were a curious or precocious kid like myself, you could never get enough of those family stories. They are pure gold to me now, as I turn my memories into books.

My mother's people were great storytellers and dream Keepers, cordoned off as they were in a small Appalachian valley, shut in by the surrounding mountains. Life was simple there. Some of the mountain folk never wandered further afield more than fifty miles in their entire lifetimes.

But something else was afoot! My people were what their English forebearers deemed Fey. They had a "Sight" as their neighbors would say.

My own grandma, Tina Bell, born blind in one eye with a large Port-wine birthmark covering part of one cheek, was especially gifted! She saw more with one eye than most folks will ever see with two. She saw into people, and through their lies and foibles and phoniness.

The end of the 18th century found Grandpa Burt cutting virgin forests along the New River, so that the new badly needed roads could be opened up.

Meanwhile Tina Bell was raising their brood of six kids, keeping chickens and a milk-cow, besides keeping up her vegetable gardens. The women in my family were said to be cunning, meaning clever, resourceful and independent. Tina Bell slept with a gun under her pillow when Burt Smith was away at his logging camp, but she had a softer, endearing side that I remember oh, so well. It seemed like yesterday when she would take my little brother on her knee and sing a few verses of "can she bake a cherry pie, Billy Boy, Billy Boy". Her time with me was even more precious. She would walk me through her sun-filled flower garden singing another ditty. "Good morning Mary Sunshine, why did you wake so soon? You chased away the little stars and shined away the moon." Gold fish, Koi, would be splashing in the water-lily pond as we circle through the flower beds. Soon her song would shift to "Mary, Mary quite contrary—how does your garden grow? With silver bells and cockle shells, and pretty maids all in a row."

These all-too brief years would form the beginning of my life-long love affair with the nature world.

As with so many other families, the great depression would force my parents to move north to the flatlands and the harsh realities of rural farm-life. My other grandmother had been a pretty Welsh girl who had married a German farmer. I mention this because it leads to an uncanny family secret: Each of my grandfathers had been born to Native American mothers. Learning of this coincidence from my parents at a young age, somehow gave me a deeper sense of belonging to the Earth. It helped me explain a small piece of the old "who am I /where did I come from" question, that most of us will eventually wrestle with; something past claiming our DNA or our genetics. There wasn't much "Tom-Foolery" on the farm. Mornings, very early—about 4:30 AM, found grandpa and my dad trudging off to the barn to do chores. Meanwhile the women-folk, grandma and my mom would be laying out the first of the three bodacious spreads of the day.

Typically, breakfast would consist of eggs, sausage, biscuits and gravy, plum preserves and potatoes fried in lard. It seemed to this five year old that as one meal was over, the next one was being prepared on the antique wood burning stove.

My Welsh grandma was a diminutive and energetic woman; the first to rise in the morning and the last to come to bed at night. I never remember seeing her smile, but I do remember her daily prayers to "Save us through Christ." It was during the farm years that I first heard about SIN. The pastor was of the hell and damnation mindset that thought that we were all sinners and forever doomed. I remember lying down in the church pew and putting my fingers in my ears to shut his sermons out.

I'm holding an old photograph—taken in 1901 at the Wright (Welsh) family reunion. Jesse, my strikingly good looking grandfather (think Viggo Mortensen!) stands off to the side, looking for all the world like an outcast. A slouch hat is pulled down over his forehead, and he seems to be ignoring the others.

I remember how in the 1930's, I would stand watching through the curtains as my grandfather was "showing" his prize Belgian stallion to a rapt circle of other farmers. Jesse knew his horses so well that he became a judge at the Ohio State fair. My dad on the other hand, hated the farm. He said he'd "Shoveled enough horse shit as a kid to last him a lifetime". He also told me how vehemently he hated churches because pastor always showed up at their table on Sunday, to claim— "The best part"—the breast of chicken. He said he was a grown man before he knew the chicken had any parts other than the back.

My dad's whimsical sense of humor may have come from the Welch side, because I can tell you, no one else in the Emerick family shared his outrageous sense of the ridiculous.

# Owl

The year was 1938. It is winter on the farm. My dad and grandpa have gone out to the barn, attending to their morning chores, when suddenly we heard the back door open. They came through the house, carefully walking sideways through the doorways. I saw them carrying something—a barn owl—by its wings. It dangled passively between them. They had brought the owl into the house to show us kids. (At the time I was four and my little brother Billy was two.)

I thought I had never seen anything so beautiful! Her large amber eyes seemed to lock into mine for one long moment, but I hoped that moment would last forever. All too soon the men turned and headed back to the barn. There, they would release the owl—an old friend of theirs who kept Grandpa's barn free of mice. That moment is forever imprinted in my mind. To this day, the owl remains my "Totem Animal".

My little brother Billy and I are standing on the first rung of the split rail fence at the side of Grandpa Jesse's barn. It must have been in the fall, because as I recall, the menfolk are butchering a hog. As I gaze off into the distance, so broad were my grandpa's fields that any other farmsteads are lost beyond our sight. In the center of the field stands one lone, tall walnut tree. It has been left standing as a "Thank offering" to the earth, in the same way the last sheath of wheat, or sheath of corn were left standing in the pagan times of Old Europe. Those farmers, sons of immigrants, still kept to the old ways.

# The Ancestors

Everyone seems to be interested in their Ancestors, but I question if the study of Genealogy has not gone far enough. Yes, it has the dates and places right, but I wish I could carry it a little deeper, to humanize these ancestors! Who were these people? What gave them joy? What was their biggest achievement? But most of all, what sort of deity did they worship?

It is said that if we go back far enough on the Family Tree, we can scratch a shaman's back, on one of the tree's branches. This applies to everyone, not just a few. The interesting thing is that you and I "stand on the shoulders" of our ancestors. Their DNA becomes ours, handed down through the ages. Most of us have no idea about our ancestors; who or what they were!

Let me cite an example: Genghis Khan, the Mongolian conqueror of the 13th century. He left his thumbprint (and more) among the women of every territory he conquered. As his armies moved through Outer Mongolia, north into what is now Russia, the numbers of his progeny increased. Centuries before his ancestors, those with Mongolian DNA (the red race!), made their way from Russia, across the frozen Bering straits, over the Aleutian Islands and into Alaska. From there they moved down the Pacific Rim and into Washington State.

At the time we lived in Washington, I would see the local tribal people's facial resemblance to the pictures of the Siberians I had seen in books. Some anthropologists began to check the teeth of native people, on both sides, and yes!, these were Genghis Khan's ancestors, who could be traced all the way back to Mongolia.

When we have some knowledge of our own forebearers, it adds a much larger dimension to the "how and what" traits of our ancestors that have been passed down to us. The variables of our "genetic stew" are vast. But how about the ways we are "emotionally wired"? These questions are far beyond my understanding, but I shall include these musings in case you wish to "connect the dots" on you own family tree.

To paraphrase that little kid's question of long ago "who are my people?" I think I can safely guess that we, you and I, have become small parts of one huge Genetic Milkshake. For a closer inquiry into our Humanness, we shall have to turn to the metaphysical (beyond our physical selves). Perhaps we can give the child's question, as he looked up into the starry night, a second look. Perhaps the poet has a better answer: "We are stardust, we are golden, and we have to get ourselves back to the garden." *Joni Mitchell.

I am looking at another photo of my grandpa Jesse, still handsome and stately into his seventies. He has high cheekbones and is wearing bib overalls. I can remember watching him reading the weekly newspaper in Beaverdam, Ohio, when I was only four. He read haltingly, painstakingly, mouthing each word. Years later I would realize that both of my grandfathers, self-made men, had less than grade school education. Yet each of them were very successful; Grandpa Burt with his saw mill, and Grandpa Jesse with his farms and Belgian horses.

I briefly mention that Grandpa Burt had been born to a Native American mother. All the information I was given was that her name was Alcinda Brain. I visualize her as being very beautiful, something like the lovely Pocahontas. I remember being told that grandpa's parents both died in the middle of a flu epidemic, during a raging snowstorm. Ten year old Burton saddled up the family horse and rode through the deep snow to a lumber camp—where the kindly loggers took him in and fed him flap-jacks. Years later, he would own the mill.

Dad's story was more to the point. He told me, "There is an Indian in the family woodpile." Many years later my older cousin would fill in the detail, telling me "Granddad's mother was Indian. He told me himself, and I believe him!"

# CHAPTER TWO

## The Mysteries

We all are on that long and winding road, that journey we must each take in order to learn what it is to be truly human. If the ups and downs of your life seem vaguely familiar that's because you've been here many times before. As they say: "Been there. Done that."

Our lives are not a one-time shot. They are just one of the many happy returns we must make in order to get it right. That old Heaven and Hell dogma, which most of us were indoctrinated with during our early years, was conjured up many, many years (think 2000) ago to keep the masses shackled and controlled by shame and guilt.

As we come into conscious thinking and living, the shift is into a more healthy self-love. The "Old School" black-board can be erased for a fresh start.

Ask yourself would a loving creator (by whatever you might call his/her name) deliberately plague us with all these catastrophic storms of life? And there are many, such as warfare, famine, flood sickness and poverty—to continue on just boggles the mind.

Since the 1950's I've hunted the dusty libraries and musty book-stores for those rare and forgotten books that might shed a little light.

I was looking for something altogether different from what the members of my family, my community and church set forth. In fact, I've done little else during my entire lifetime than search for answers!

Whenever I've met someone more learned, wiser than myself, I've gladly "sat at their feet," soaking it up like a sponge. In the process I've met some very advanced teachers who took me in tow and shared what they had to offer. In turn, I vowed I would pass these lessons on to those who were ready to listen.

An awakening to one's higher self can come suddenly, or through several life lessons spread across time. Many factors play a part in our willingness to learn; from the adults who set an example in our childhood homes, to the influence of our early companions, or sometimes through the life partner of our choice. Progress can even come through the shock and grief of a loss. Growth comes to us through many avenues!

Always, I try to seek out those who are different. I now realize how very fortunate I was to be born into a family of Fey women in Appalachia at the height of the great depression. I listened intently whenever my mother and her sisters told their dreams over the breakfast table, or when they spoke of "Signs" or any of the magical happenings they found in their otherwise ordinary lives.

Within a more pragmatic family, the sensitive child might suffer ridicule if he shows his mystical bent. How fortunate is the child who is allowed to develop a love for the nature world unhampered; free to look for faeries under every toadstool!

Do you ever feel that this generation of children is overburdened with too much homework or too many extra-curricular activities? Where can they find any time for solitude or for dreaming? We do not encourage the solitude that's needed for a rich inner life in our society. It seems the dreamer, or the visionary, the one who "is different", is always chastised.

Look at what the astronomers Keplar and Copernicus had to endure for watching the night sky! To say the earth was not flat or that it actually revolved around the sun was very dangerous in those times! Those who had the gift of foresight, or other psychic abilities, were hounded by the church, and often punished by imprisonment or by burning at the stake. This horrendous period of the dark ages has been mostly swept under the rug. Just as much as the errant behavior of rogue priests who have tormented the children in their charge.

Yet most of the ancient mysteries, those called Earth Magic, have prevailed. For example, the experienced gardeners know enough to plant root vegetables in the Dark of the Moon. The farmer knows instinctively when the "time is right" to burn off his fields, to plant and when to harvest. These earth-wisdoms are unique!

Somewhere, dreams are still being recited within a family of dreamers, and old farm-wives still remember how to make a mustard plaster for the child with "The croup:" We know the buzzards will return to Hinkly Ohio on March 15th, just as sure as swans will return to Michigan's upper peninsula to build their nests and lay their eggs. All this is part of grand design. Known to but "The few," those with a rich inner life.

The first time I saw a Luna moth being carried in the beak of a bird, I was sure I was seeing a Faerie in the diaphanous pale green grown, who had been captured and was now struggling with all her might to escape. Let me confess, I was not still a child at this

11

magical sighting, but a middle-aged grandma caught up in the magic of the moment. Those who had parents who read "the Blue Faerie" books to them will understand. We never outgrow that magical world.

# Isolation

Let me share a story that sheds light on the damage of isolation. Children need companions, and animals are much the same. My daughter is an equestrian who does horse rescue. Five years ago she took in a towering (17.2 hands) chestnut racehorse. On his maiden race he was expected to win because of his strength and size. But he failed his owner's expectations. From that day forward Beau Jorge was locked up alone in his stall. He was fed and watered but never let out to be with his stable-mates, or feel the green grass beneath his feet.

Beau Jorge pined away, distraught by his isolation. When my daughter took him home, as a "rescue", he slowly came back to himself. With the patience of his new owner, and the freedom to graze with the other horses, he thrived.

Children who are neglected can also languish. Without touch, gentle rocking or other human contact they fail to thrive. In extreme cases they may even lose their will to live. Those who take in animals or who care for children in need are "Angels in Waiting", at least in my book!

So how does that child, the one who is gifted with whimsical fantasies, or the one who is born with a knack for telling dreams become able to navigate this sensible world? In many cases he will bloom into a poet, an artist, a writer, or movie director! But I can tell you first hand, that such Fey (Faerie-like) or weird talents are not always welcome outside the limited households where the child will be cherished and his gifts will be accepted.

I'm thinking of Carl Jung, a pioneer in his field of psychoanalysis, who shared his childhood memories—to be published only after his death. It is an example of a Fey, acutely sensitive child, born into a family of practical, no-nonsense persons who will expect him to follow suit. As an adult Carl Jung excelled beyond all expectations, but it was his childhood memoirs that held my attention! His disclosures struck a nerve!

I could relate because I was also a quirky child—lost in imaginings and daydreams, unable to deal with the realities of mathematics or science, but a whiz at memorizing passages from Shakespeare. Books were my salvation; especially anything with a mystical bent. It took a long time to find a teacher! I was well into my thirties when not just one, but two esoteric teachers would appear. Both were steeped in the metaphysical wisdom I was searching for.

They shored up my confidence and taught me it was alright to be myself. My first teacher, Bertha, informed me "You are a super sensitive, who will someday do my work!" When I met my next teacher, John, he told me "You are a mystic out of this world"! Heady stuff from the two people who made all the difference

To those with a mystical bent, I would suggest you find a good teacher. Another possibility is to join a mystery school, such as B.O.T.A., the Rosicrucian's, or the Order of the Golden Dawn. There are several good teaching centers out there, available at a decent cost. Have someone knowledgeable refer you! Your other course of action would be to read, learn and follow your innate intuition. (I know a man who actually did this!)

As I look ahead to my eighties, I see more study before me, blended with my daily meditations. Our universe is massive, and spirit is to be found everywhere. It may be that you will choose to discard some of those old notions in order to move forward. Even a lifetime of study can't scratch the surface. But remember, you are building on your efforts from many past lifetimes and will have your teachers from the past anxious to assist you.

When people first walked on the moon, just a few generations ago, they brought back samples from outer space that proved the composition of the moon and stars holds the same elements that are found in our human bodies. Are we, indeed, cells of the Cosmic Whole? Or, as the Bible puts it—"Are we created a little lower than the Angels?" Never discount the possibilities as you prepare to launch yourself into the study of the mysteries.

# CHAPTER THREE

## The Primitives

Some random thoughts about the spirit worlds as I envision them at this stage of my development are as follows:

The spirit worlds seem to be multiple layers, perhaps existing just above or within our earth-reality. This place—or these places—are a reality that exists as a cosmic stopover between our successive earth-visits. Such a respite encompasses the spirits of those who have passed over, where it serves as a sort of rest and recuperative station.

My understanding is that there is a temple of learning there, where we can observe our past deeds, and reflect on the ways we can hone our soul's growth in a future lifetime. As the voice (channeled) of my birth father reported—"We are closer than hands and feet!"

For those who have had a prolonged period of suffering prior to the death experience, there is also a temple of healing. Here, the soul rests until it is healed and strong enough for re-entry (birth) into human form.

There is an enormous choice of possibilities on this subject, drawn from several cultures which extend back through the ages. Let's begin our journey back through time with a look into pre-history and the "first people."

Following the path of evolution, science tells us that the fore-runners of our human race would eventually stand up (bi-pedal) on their back feet and begin to fashion some crude tools. Early man, "the primitives" may have had a basic awareness of their own death, along with their basic perception of a "Life source". This is borne out by artifacts and burial practices. We know the Ancient Ones lived up close and personal with danger in a scary landscape that offered death at every hand.

Buffeted by raging storms and pursued by hungry, oversized predators, nature itself must have been intimidating. A stroke of lightening could set the veld aflame, while a gentle rain would produce tubers and other foods for the hunter/gatherers. Early people stood under the same canopy of stars, that same night sky, as ourselves. Could they, at some early stage of their development, even begin to form a thought about where they "came from"? I doubt it! For the primitives, their needs were simple, but urgent. The basic need was to survive in a hostile landscape where life interfaced with death on a daily basis.

Let's fast-forward now to a time where people gathered in tribal groups around a campfire. Language skills have now developed to the point where they can engage in storytelling. (Story telling is an art still used among tribal people around the world.) I fondly remember an evening of storytelling among the S'Klallam people in northwest Washington. This is how the early people came together to relate the legends and myths of their past. Among their legends would be tales of Genesis, i.e. "this is how we arrived here!" The eastern (woodland) tribes believe we descended from the stars as "Star-sperm." While the desert tribes of the west's Four-corners tell their story in this way; "We came up from the Sipapu, the belly button of mother earth. And so today, they enter the underground Kiva to do ceremony.

Somewhere around 500 BC, the Greeks, Romans and Vikings were each creating their pantheons of gods and goddesses. They created them in their own human images; in mythic, bigger-than-life figures, who like themselves waged battles, slew their enemies and made off with beautiful women! They even gave names to the stars above, linking Mars with the god of war, or Venus as the goddess of beauty, etc, thus creating their gods and goddesses into figures like themselves.

Meanwhile, on the British Isles, an array of whimsical little people would develop. The magical Nature Sprites; faeries, elves, gnomes, and the like; are still found in storybooks. India has its own angelic Divas and an estimated 350,000 (check it out!) gods and goddesses according to mythologist Joseph Campbell. The Druids, the white-robed priests of the Celts were educated, with an advanced culture by the time Julius Caesar arrived on the scene. They had an alphabet, a language, knowledge of plant-based medicine, and elaborate burial rituals-believing their dead would continue to live on in a nether-world. The Vikings to the north called it Valhalla, and the witches and other pagans named their afterlife "The Summer-land".

Now we turn to a brief look at tribal peoples of North America, all of whom made Spirit an integral part of their lives A warrior would affirm "this is a good day to die," as he stood in mortal battle. They saw Great Spirit as it manifested in the natural world around them. Death came as part of the Great Mystery of Life, because they described their ancestors as resting only three days walk from the Land of the Living: meaning "close at hand; not too far away." So here we see a sampling of the beliefs of our indigenous people who had an inkling of immortality. Who believed their souls would survive beyond death, in the spirit-lands.

# The Great Migrations

The location of the very first people seems up for grabs according to Mary and Louis Leaky, a family of Anthropologists. They seem to be best known for excavating a "dig" in the Olduvai Gorge in Africa, which scientists dated as 100,000 years old. Other Archeologists have placed the first people in the fertile crescent of Mesopotamia, long referred to as the "Cradle of Civilization". Another find was Peking Man, in China. So, with each new discovery, the dawn of civilization is constantly shifting over the ages.

What we do know is that the first people evolved from Hominids, who were very short, but stood upright (called bi-pedal) and who were using simple tools. Some new discoveries will certainly pop-up in the future to change all the records. Those earliest people were extremely basic in their needs, which were food and shelter, and a need to procreate their species. Without meeting these basic requirements, the human race would have petered out long ago.

But our Ancient People were amazingly resilient, strong and clever. The first people stood in awe of the night sky, the storms, floods, brush fires and predator animals, just as we do today. Only just recently I learned that the Red Race of man originated in Mongolia! Each piece of information is another piece of the puzzle that had brought us to this place and time!

Every Root Race: red, black, yellow and white have handed down their genesis stories. Among these creation myths runs the common thread of the Great Migrations. If the Ancient ones could speak, they might tell us "We started over there. We moved to here." A mixing of the tribes was also fostered during these long migrations, as groups of people moved south to warmer climates and a more abundant supply of game.

We know that birds chart their spring and fall migrations according to the slant of the sun. Lobsters, on the floor of the oceans will follow the phases of the moon through the dark and shifting waters. In movement, as in migrations, everything is interactive.

The Anasazi, a forerunner of today's Pueblo people, claimed they emerged from underground, then moved in circular migrations to populate the whole earth. Every ancient people claim their own "Genesis" story. But with oral traditions, passed down through word of mouth, parts of each story will be embellished, and other parts will be altered or left out, altogether!

Let's move to South America, where there are etchings of what appears to be ancient astronauts on the earth. These figures are so large they can be more easily seen from the air! Legends say these etchings were left by the Beings from outer space. Mayan predictions for the year 2012 tell us that we are now in the time period when such extraterrestrial beings will once again make contact. Large numbers of both astrologers and psychics are watching carefully for such developments.

But as I write I find I am even more interested in another type of migration, one which traces back to the question from the little girl standing beneath a starry night sky.

Who am I? Where did I come from? The Hindu people believed in what they call "Transmigration of Souls". That each of us is in his/her process of spiritual evolution, form one level to the next. This mirrors the "climb" up the tree of life, within the Kabbalah, and the kindness (Metta) to not harm "All sentient beings" according to the Buddhist doctrine. In this way we are able to advance, and to gain merit.

# CHAPTER FOUR

## "The Entities"

The year was 1971. I had just come through a drawn-out divorce and was ready for a new beginning. I was ready to try many new things in an effort to come into balance. In this process I attended some of the Spiritualist churches and sat through two sessions with the transcendentalist meditators. I also began haunting the Metaphysical book-stores to see what was out there. Sometimes I felt I was in training, not for a race, but for a spiritual breakthrough. I needed some answers!

After my first astrology reading, with a well-known reader, I felt a glimmer of hope for the future. Whenever I let my guard down, closed my eyes, and entered meditation, I could feel a shift of awareness. Only a newcomer to meditation, I had no idea that it would open the floodgates to my inherent psychic abilities.

My routine was simply to sit cross-legged on my bed in silent meditation. What happened on one ordinary summer's day was totally unexpected. I had barely entered the meditative state, when the long face of a regal-looking East Indian wearing a white turban appeared about three feet away. He had a white beard and was looking at me with an intense gaze.

"Who are you?" I asked mind-to-mind. He held up a square white poster-board with a lovely scripted letters I could not identify. It was a very stylized lettering with artful rises and dips. Then suddenly the vision faded. I felt I had briefly wandered into alien territory—a place or time I was not yet prepared for.

But soon after this first experience I began having a series of spirit visitors who were beyond imagination. The next image to appear was that of a Cardinal. (I'm guessing, here.) But he was wearing a red robe and a tall, pointy hat. I asked—again, mind-to-mind, who he was, and heard (inside my head) "Father Joseph". He reminded me that very recently, when I had swerved my car to avoid an accident, he had protected me.

It didn't stop there! In close sequence there would appear a harem dancing girl in silk pantaloons. "Who are you?" I asked. And she told me: "I am you, long ago." Instantly it came to me that perhaps I had lived a life as a courtesan in a far-away desert country. Why were these figures from the past coming to me? I felt unhinged! "What's happening to me?", I asked my teacher.

"You are having a psychic meltdown, that's all." John assured me. "It happens, sometimes triggered by a crisis in your life. You suddenly break free of the constraints of your once three-dimensional world. All at once you realize there are no barriers in time and space—between whom you once were and who you are now. You have the same soul, just wearing a series of personalities in different time frames, He explained.

What would I have done without my teacher's wise guidance? He placed some out-of-print books in my hands, about how the universe works. What I gleaned from them was that the Kabbalists, the Universalists and the Theosophists were not so far apart in their teachings. In those early years as a student, I often ran across material that was too esoteric for me to decipher. The word "occult" means all things hidden. The masters of Metaphysics (beyond the physical) obviously weren't writing to, or leaving behind, their secrets for the dabblers! They had fashioned a system of "blinds" and detours to eliminate the student who was not truly committed to the pursuit of truth and wisdom.

About this time I found myself in a strange dream. In it, I was walking around the campus of Toledo University. On the second story of one of the stone buildings was a large, round stained-glass window with a colorful flower-shaped design. In my dream, I levitated off the ground, and broke through, shattering that same window. Fragments of glass flew everywhere! Now I was inside a classroom. Seated around a long table was an assembled group of twenty or so elderly men. Within my dream I realized I had happened upon a group of Master Teachers; the "Mages" from the past. They all wore robes with hoods pushed back, as you would find in a secret society. Looking back forty years later, I believe there are legions of master teachers operating in a higher dimension to assist those who struggle toward enlightenment.

Perhaps the most important book my teacher gave me during those early years deserves mention. It was "The Mystical Qaballa" by Dion Fortune, first published in London in 1935. I've found it to be the very best source for the study of the Tree of Life.

I am remembering how, in that small pocket of time, so many opportunities were presenting themselves. There will never be any more perfection in the sequence of events, as they happened in the summer of 1971!

# The Mediums

Small Metaphysical groups were forming around Toledo. One group I sat with was using a Ouija Board. But there random messages I observed seemed to be haphazard and superficial. Soon I moved to join three other people at another card table.

They motioned for me to sit down in the empty chair, evidently because they needed one more person to levitate the table. We each placed our hands, palms down on the surface of the table. To my surprise it wobbled once or twice, and then raised itself about two inches off the floor. This happened in a well-lit room, so there was no mistaking what had occurred.

When I asked my teacher John about it, he said; "Phenomena are happening all the time. It's all about energy! If you can get your "Thinking mind" out of the way, you can accomplish anything!"

Things were moving very fast! Soon afterward I was invited to "sit" with a group of "Developing Mediums". Curious to understand more about how spirit manifests in this five-sense world I jumped at the opportunity. The other women were already seated at the circular dining room table, so I took the empty chair. No sooner had the "Candle of Protection" been lit than things began to happen.

First, the light-bulbs in the overhead chandelier all went out, and I saw pin-points of light shower down around us. One woman began to tremble, and another cautioned—"Don't touch her, she's in a trance!"

The Medium then began spouting fragmented sentences—something about "Thor Heyerdahl" and "Azure Blue". I could see her appearance had changed. Her voice had deepened and tears were running down her cheeks. It was all very frightening to me—a newcomer to spiritualism and all its ensuing phenomena.

In the weeks that followed we continued to meet for séances, but we moved the location to my house as the numbers of curious increased. I kept a pad and pencil ready as the message would come through the medium. She would say, tell the scribe (myself) "this or that" and I would write it down. Sometimes there would be a flurry—as those on the other side tried to come through. Interestingly, one session was filled with accounts of bombings to a convent during world war II. We heard from many spirits, but the message of most interest to me included my father along with his older brother "Marcus Lyle", described as wearing bib overalls. (Uncle Marcus had been a dairy farmer during his lifetime.) If I had ever been a skeptic before this, the references from my father—things only he could know—dispelled any doubts that our spirits live on!

I continued holding séances and also visiting spiritualist mediums throughout that year. Some of the Mediums urged me to join them in doing the work of an "Open Channel" to the other side. But once again, I resisted. It was tempting, but I had the idea of creating a Teaching Center in the back of my mind. What the Spirits taught me, in their words was "We are all around you. We are closer than hands and feet!"

It was a busy time, but whenever I could reach a deeper level of meditation, one of the Entities would appear. Some of my visitors had once spent their lifetimes in the public spotlight. I remember that one was Teddy Roosevelt, and another was Mark Twain. When I spoke of the contacts to my teacher, John, he suggested that I was "Rising on the Plains". He urged me to return to the study of Kabbalah, in order to (in his words) "Keep myself Grounded."

# Kabbalah

This will be a simplified description in which I will introduce four of the Tree of Life's better known Archangels:

I want to describe the Tree of Life as a "Stairway to the Stars". The Kabbalah has stood the test of time for roughly three to five thousand years. It is considered by many to be the most comprehensible diagram of the universe. When my teacher placed his book in my hands, he warned me not to read Dion Fortunes "Mystical Qabalah" all in one sitting, of course he was joking! I'm still working the paths and making new discoveries more than forty years later.

The Ascent of the Tree begins right here on Earth; solid ground, terra firma. From here we travel to the moon, where the element is water and the archangel contact is Gabriel.

Next we move to the planet Venus. The element is Earth (think nature world) and the archangel is Uriel. Arriving at the Sun-center, the element is Fire and the Archangel is Michael. The planet Mercury represents the Air, and the Archangel here is Raphael. This is a brief introduction to the core references for the beginner, which as we advance, is useful for rising on the plains This is a serious body of work in itself, but perhaps this sampling will tweak your curiosity to investigate it further, on your own!

Astrology, including the seven (first known) planets and the twelve houses of the Zodiac was also well known, not only to the Kabbalists, but to other advanced scholars over time. During the years I was actively teaching Metaphysics, I would offer a course in Astrology, then introduce the Tarot Cards, and last of all offer Kabbalah in a course I called "Up the Tree". These three subjects form the foundation of the western Esoteric system of study. Of course the other possibilities are endless. It is always my hope that the Reader will "venture forth" to enrich both his mind and his spirit.

# Astral Projection

This too was a subject of quite a lot of attention during the early seventies. Various teachers were presenting exercises that could lead to "Distant Viewing" also called "travel in the Vision-mind". It is said in the Zohar, on this subject, "when a person is sleeping in his bed, his soul leaves the body and meets with those in the spirit world". In my research I found this theme in various other sources, including an excellent dog-eared book titled "Invisible Healers" by C.W. Leadbeatter, first published in London in 1896. Elsewhere this phenomenon is referred to as "Travel in the Night Vision". A few of my students have spoken about the feeling of "Falling back in their bodies with a jolt". It gives a convincing argument, that so many references detail the ability to bi-locate and to bring accounts of the people and places they have seen back! Some give descriptions of a Guardian or Guide who will accompany them on their out-of-body experiences.

My opinion is that various Angelic Beings of the shining light in Kabbalism, such as "Shekinah" (also spelled Schenchina), known in the Judaic as the divine feminine presence, are similar to the Shakti in Hindu sources. At any rate Angelic helpers from many orders will be closely identified from our human perspective. The Shekinah "Carries a mystical capacity" that she can bring to mankind. You will see the references to Shekinah, the moon and the angelic helpers mentioned throughout these pages.

Our planet Earth is where we incarnate (come into a lifetime) in order to learn what it is to be truly human. This is where we learn through our own failures and "hard knocks" to have compassion for others, as they become more enlightened through their own human mistakes! So, you see, we are all in the same boat; we come here, we learn, and we evolve spiritually. Earth can be considered the Kindergarten, at least in our solar system.

## Energies of the Sun and Moon

Directly above us and orbiting around the Earth is our moon; also called Yesod or Luna. The moon is a filter-down or, "Repository" for the energies of all the other planets. You might describe the moon as the big "Garage Sale in the sky" it is the receptacle for impressions, dreams, and for the "Fey", psychic impressions. To Yesod we assign the element of water, moveable and quickly changing, like a woman. The moon directs the ebb and flow of the sea, as well as the emotions and fertility cycles of women. Yesod's Archangel is Gabriel, as mentioned.

As the moon is feminine, the energy of our sun is considered masculine. The sun-center of our universe is known in the Hebraic as Tiphareth. Science tells us that the sun spots on the surface of the sun will trigger earthquakes on our planet. Esoteric wisdom assigns the color gold, and the energy of our solar-plexus chakra to the ego—self identification, the "I am". All of us struggle with this ego-self identification. In some cases, with athletes and other performers, it can express through unhealthy or overbearing cycles, against the loss of the spiritual self when we have an emotional set-back. Without the positive influences of Tiphareth, we would not dare to become the "Best that is in us", in the spiritual sense. Tiphareth calls out to those who are prepared to give of themselves for the good of many. The Jesus, The Buddha, or the other pure souls who visit Earth as Human Avatars.

# Ancient Astronomers

Let's go to the Middle East. One highly developed people were the Persians. They created a large empire that spread over most of the mid-east. In our times Persia is known as Iraq. Although we may think of Persia as the land of Genies and magic carpets, it was a significant center of learning prior to the 350 B.C.E. The three wise men from the East, who visited the baby Jesus in the manger, were Persian Astrologers. The star they followed to Bethlehem is now thought to be a conjunction of the planets Jupiter and Saturn by some astrologers. For thousands of years prior to our time frame, people have felt a connection to and an influence from the stars.

I have come to believe that each one of us has a vibrational connection with the way the planets fall in the respective houses of the Zodiac at the time of our birth. As an Astrologer, I also believe we are influenced in our "psychic wiring" by these planetary placements. The configuration of the planets can influence our behavior patterns, our strengths and weaknesses as well as some basic choices we will make during our lifetimes. We look at these "Tendencies."

Having spent forty years drawing up and interpreting horoscopes, I have come to trust the positions of the stars. This is a map; the influences are there! Some of you will be born leaders, others will be creative or artistic. The very sensitive or those who march to a different drum will reject the norms of what society dictates we should do. Each person is unique, with their own special talents, abilities, and choices they will make.

But now, let me go a step beyond astrology. We have no idea what the soul, within the person, might have achieved prior to this lifetime. They may have been a humanitarian, or a scoundrel, or any manner of things in-between. It could be a history of good deeds, or a load of negative baggage, according to the laws of karma. I realize that what I'm saying here may be outside your comfort zone, so let me remind you that about two thirds of the world's population embraces the possibility of reincarnation. (If you want more on this subject, I might suggest you read "Old Souls" by Tom Shroder.)

We are complex people—each one of us a bundle of contradictions. We each have our own riddles to unravel. For myself, that's what makes "another chance", another lifetime so promising!

From the ancient astrologers of Persia to the modern technology of today, we have clocked the planet's spirals through space with the most exacting accuracy. Scienists can tell us about the alignments of the sun, moon and stars. And, on a clear night we can us a telescope, or even view the stars with our naked eye! Eclipses will still send chickens running toward hen houses and cause milk cows to head for the barn. Such is the way of our interconnecting universe.

# Buddhism

This peaceful belief system has taken the world by storm. (Sorry, no pun intended.) Since the 1970's when Chogyam Trungpa brought it to America, it has spread world-wide. This is a practice of meditation, study, and kindness shown to all living creatures. A teacher is very helpful, as are retreats, and a host of books to be found in many bookstores as well as on-line. But for the solitary meditator like myself, who buys books and documentaries, the practice can still be life-changing.

I was first drawn to Buddhism because #1, The Buddhists seemed so peaceful within themselves, and #2, They do not fear death! They see both birth and death as parts of the ongoing wheel, which is always turning. One practitioner said: "Ours is a subtle world, not at all solid as many would imagine. When a song is over, does it linger in a room? If we walk across the floor, do the footprints remain?"

Buddhists show kindness to all living creatures, and live simple but rich inner lives. That we come from spirit and return to spirit is something accepted for thousands of years by many who practice Eastern philosophies. They already know that life on earth is harsh. So some hold to the idea that we should weep when a new soul comes into this plane of dense matter and rejoice when they escape the bonds of Earth-existence. My practice is simple:

Upon awakening, I first express my gratitude. Thus begins the day. Then I join with untold others in prayer for those who suffer.

31

Sometimes I might light a candle on my altar on behalf of someone who is ill or bereaved. Or, offer up a healing prayer.

The "OM" is the universal sound of life! The repeated sound of the "OM" will immediately lift the vibration of any room. The sound of Tibetan Bowls or a stick of fragrant incense serves to remind us that we are connected to everyone else on the pathways of life.

# CHAPTER FIVE

## 2012 "The Mayans"

The word that comes to mind is Metamorphosis! As we neared year 2012 there was excitement in the air. My astrologer friends, along with the mystics and scholars around the world, were all putting their guesses out there.

"What will happen" we asked one another "when the Mayan calendar runs out of pages on December 21st, 2012?" "Will this create another Big Bang?" "Will a new era of peace and brotherhood begin?" "Will dictatorships around the world suddenly collapse?"

As a Tarot card reader, the card in the Taro deck that fit the times was Major Arcana #16, "The Tower." We had already seen the big money changers on Wall Street come to scandal in 2008. Banks were making loans to folks who could not make the payments on their new house. Greedy bankers could then repossess those properties and put them up for sale again. Yes! We found ourselves in the worst recession since the 1930's—and this was the second one in my own lifetime!

The Tower Card in the Tarot is one of calamity. A bolt of lightning has struck a high tower, setting it on fire. Foundation shattered, the tower is in a state of collapse. Desperate people fall (or jump) from the windows. The card's meaning in a nutshell is "The overthrow of old systems".

When I asked my friend what would follow, he told me one word "Adjustment"! American soldiers were back in Afghanistan, engaged in an endless war that even the experts had deemed unwinnable. Back home we had the jobless on one hand and the "Occupy America" homeless in the public parks. Many of the couples in my age-bracket were opting to down-size, while everyone struggled to adjust to the changes.

The new age, said to last 26,000 years is ushering in the 5th wave of humanity. This could be the Age of Aquarius, an opening in time for the age of brotherhood to emerge. But is humankind ready? I dwell on this brief segment of our recent history in order to set the scene for what was to follow.

# The Insects

It is a cold night in mid-January in northwest Ohio. Temperatures are sub-zero. Just before dark, Frank has trudged out into the snow to fill all five of our bird feeders. This is what we call a winter-kill for the birds. I pull the blankets up to my chin, wondering how anything can survive in the cold and wind.

Sometime during the night I wake up. Something small and alive is sitting on my heart chakra—on top of my gown. I quickly switch on the light to discover it is a lady-bug. These are my favorite little orange polka-dot beetles. They often winter-over in our house until spring—when I will carry each one outside to a fresh new start.

Very shortly afterward I had a second such incident. This time I woke up on another cold and blustery night. The first thing I noticed was that the room smelled wonderfully green and fresh, like a newly cut lawn. When I switched on the light, a small black insect was sitting on my heart chakra, looking up into my face. It was what my mother always referred to as a "Box Elder" bug.

Where did these little messengers come from, and why? They would set off a series of happenings that would change my life in the years between 2010 and 2012.

I do know that after my little visitors came to me there was a subtle shift in my heart; thought to be the "Seat of the Soul" by the Ancients. I became kinder, more patient than before. I wanted to be a better person. I was waiting for a direct assignment from the universe!

# Visitation

Winter melted into spring. What happened next was totally unexpected. I will recount it as accurately as possible from my journal entry.

Again, I am asleep in my bed, when a soft stirring brought me awake. The room was dim, but not dark. I sat up to see. Five feet from the foot of my bed was a figure. She was "big as life" wearing a pale yellow gown, not unlike the nightgown I was wearing. I attempted to call out to my husband but my voice was gone. About this time the figure was starting to fade. I called out again, not in fear but in surprise. My husband's door was closed, so he did not hear my call. When I attempted to get out of bed, the floor under my feet felt like it was rising and falling like waves of water. I was unsteady on my feet. By now a new thought entered my mind. Perhaps I had died and an angel had come for me.

It took me a few minutes to get to the living room, turning on lights as I shakily moved to the couch. When my husband came downstairs I told him in a still weak voice that I was dying. I asked him not to call 911, because for some strange reason I was not afraid. Then I told him about the entity in my room.

I thought about canceling my class the next morning. What reason could I give? "Sorry girls, I had an angel here last night?" But as I met the ladies at the door, I found I couldn't remember some of their names. So, I explained by telling the group about my angelic visitation—for want of a better name.

Someone suggested I had left my body and was having trouble slipping back in. Another person said the figure might have been my "Astral self" or "Mirror image". So we discussed the possibilities. In the days ahead I'd give the entity a name. I called her "Divine Shekinah". To me she represents the divine feminine aspect of the sacred. Whatever her name, I felt somehow different, lighter, more fragile and vulnerable.

Something had changed. In the weeks that followed I felt a deeper awareness of the Entities. They were continuing to move through my room, usually between 3:15-3:30 AM. "They" (by now I realized these were various entities, not just one) come with a pale-blue hue: something I would describe as a moon-beam.

I have come to understand that angels in no way come to frighten me. In fact they carry with them a comfortable ambiance as they pass through our surroundings. I also believe they are with us, You and I, in close proximity, to uplift and inspire us during an energy exchange. As we develop our ability to receive these exchanges we grow more comfortable with the concept that spirit is all around us.

In esoteric studies we are taught there are both "senders" and "receivers" of subtle impressions. When I sense a presence, I used those brief moments to speak silent prayers of gratitude. Sometimes I send love to my departed kin, or less often, to ask for guidance on my own spiritual journey. One thing I feel/hear them urging me to do is to work with the bereaved. Most importantly those who suffer with unmitigated grief, because their emotions can hamper their loved one's adjustment on the other side. I also can feel the help of unseen helpers as I attempt to write this book. Our invisible helpers are advanced beings that have the ability to travel through space and time to where they are most needed. If we condition ourselves to be receptive they will enter in the silence and pale-blue darkness to bring peace.

## From the Poets

We have not come here to take prisoners but to surrender ever more deeply to freedom and joy.
> Run my dear
> From anything
> That may not strengthen
> Your precious budding wings

For we have come here not to take prisoners or to confine our wondrous spirits but to experience.

Ever and ever more deeply our divine courage, freedom and light.
> . . . the poet Hafiz

Or, from another poet—
"Progress is impossible without change, and those who cannot change their minds cannot change anything."
> . . . Ralph Waldo Emerson

And, another—
> "Who, if I cried out,
> Would hear me,
> In the orders of angels?"
> . . . R.M Rilke

Note: The writers and poets throughout time have had the ability to inspire us and to lift us up from our mundane lives. O.W.

# Simpler Lifestyle

We all want to be well and there are many ways to be there. Have you heard of Ayurveda? It is ancient Hindu type of lifestyle which is now becoming popular in America as well. This system restores joy, health, and wisdom to the body and mind through herbs, teas, ointments, and natural foods. Ayurveda also incorporates rituals such as dance, drumming chant and song in its holistic lifestyle.

Sometimes, when we are stressed, we will crave the very "treat", that is bad for us. For me it's chocolate! For others it could be tobacco or alcohol. Pick your poison! Every time I purchase a box of "Russell Stover" candy an alarm goes off; my personal "Jimminy Cricket". But that small voice could also be called "The knower within, or the witness, or the Higher self. "They" can let you know when your diet or an addiction is making you ill. Stress of all kinds is running rampant in our society and can ruin your health. Listen to that small voice when you feel your body-energies are off.

The simpler our lifestyle—the healthier we become. Many Americans abuse their health by over-eating and not getting enough sleep! Late-night TV and those addictive computer games can wear us down. At our house, we make it a habit to wind-down as it gets dark, and to arise with the dawn. We are also careful to have a very light meal several hours before bedtime.

# Grief Seminar

"Such is the meaning of time, it's too fast to fold" says songwriter Eddie Vedder. There is no way to slow it down. "There is no death, only a change of worlds" spoke Chief Seattle.

Yet most of us caught in the pervasive mindset of our culture's dominant belief system have a difficult time making friends with death. Is it because, to many, death seems so permanent?

But to those who suffer through a lingering, painful illness, death may loom as a welcomed friend! It all depends on our conditioning.

"We should grieve when we come into this Earth reality and celebrate when we leave." said someone well-acquainted with that cycle we each will go through. This seems to be the case in many eastern cultures where life and death interface on a daily basis.

Separation from a loved one is always difficult, without question. But, it helps to remember that we mourn for ourselves, not the departed. Those who grieve on and on, even to the point of a physical breakdown, do the deceased loved one no favors. Spiritualist teachings describe it this way:

Once on the other side, called Bardo plane, the recently dead is faced with the assignment of ADJUSTMENT. For a time they will exist in a weightless body in this border state (known as the "Bardo" to the Tibetans). The survivor's grief can hold their loved one back. When we mourn excessively or over-long this keeps the newly dead from moving on to their next assignment. There are angelic teachers and healers on the other side who will help the departed soul to make their adjustments—those necessary for their next re-entry!

If you wish to help (assist) the departed in the adjustment stages, the following are some guide-lines:

To _____(name) say—
"My dear one, I congratulate you who are in a new and better place! I will someday join you in that place where time stands still.

Thank you for all the joy your lifetime has brought into my life. I will remember your earth walk with great gratitude. I see you smiling, free from anxiety, and now surrounded by your guides and guardians. I will always remember you _____(name) with positive thoughts and gladness."

Note to the Bereaved:

Now, let go of any selfish clinging on your part. Let the loved one's spirit "fly free", and do not attempt to hold him/her back. Life and death are both parts of the divine process. We knew this when were in the "Floating process" prior to our own human birth experience. We shall realize it once again when we step out of this "heavy human overcoat" which we think of as our body. Accepting these teachings from those who have gone before us will help you understand the complete life experience.

Some things you can do—instead of grieving—which will benefit both yourself and humanity are to:

- Follow the guidelines on the prior pages. Re-read them as often as needed. Forget that old conditioning!
- Become consciously aware when you fool yourself slipping back into old patterns of obsession.
- Do something for others! This will enlarge not only your world view, but your circle of friendships. Move beyond family members!

- Choose a cause! If you are in good health, volunteer at a food bank or soup kitchen.
- Take a walk. Invite a neighbor in for tea (and do not obsess while they are there!) Fight against the impulse.
- Plant a "memorial tree" in your loved person's honor.
- Plant a memorial garden of flowers.
- Take a class, replace your grief with a meaningful activity.
- Smile when you think of "your person". Look at their lifetime as a gift from above.

# Discontent

Absolute power corrupts absolutely! We see this in war-torn dictatorships in today's world. We see it on Wall Street with the big money-changers we see it in "tent-cities" for the homeless.

It has always been thus. Going back 2000 years people were under the yoke of the powerful, whenever someone new came on the scene. Jesus was a Rabbi; a teacher and a good man. He did not set out to found a church, only to speak of kindness in a very dark period of history. But what happened in the five centuries following his death was what so often happens within large institutions. Jesus' words, passed down by oral tradition, did not come to us intact, or as intended. Luke (the physician) was the only apostle who could read and write. The rest was hear-say; some of it was not written down until 300 A.D. As the church grew, it became the world's largest landowner. (It was the nature of things to steal lands from widows who could not pay taxes!)

What would Jesus say today, in our times, when various churches have become enmeshed with the goal of prosperity and abundance (meaning corruption) rather than charity?

Gautama Buddha was another good man. Like many avatars who have come to our earth to spread enlightenment, his message was kindness and mercy. Anytime the leaders of a large and prosperous institution lose track of their mission, which is to uphold the dignity of all persons, of political freedom and charity, it crumbles from within. Only those who speak with clarity and truth in our times are fit to lead. Violence and corruption have been going on since time immemorial. I did some study on the rise and fall of ancient societies only to find nothing much has changed in the way we now treat one another.

Disenchanted with churches, I turned to studies of the eastern esoteric beliefs. First, I came upon Hinduism, reading the Upanishads, then the Bhagavad Gita. Everything I was reading spoke of spirit; in the larger sense; saying spirit existed in everything. In planting a garden, in something as common as the preparation of nourishing food, in song or chant, in dance, or simply taking a walk.

# Honoring the Buddha

I follow the "Practice" but in no way do I consider myself an expert on Buddhism. I am a beginner, and as such I shall share a few basics with my readers. As a practicing Buddhist I have set up a small altar on my east wall, with crystals, a bell and a candle and images of His Holiness the 14th Dalai Lama. On the opposite wall hang five prayer flags. They represent the five elements of wind, earth, fire, air and water. This room is where I meditate, pray, and send out "petitions" on behalf of those who suffer.

In my living room, on the coffee table, I've created a Zen Garden. Mine is not made ot sand, but instead of three earth tone dishes, which help me clear my mind and connect with nature. I change my Zen Garden every day, constantly touching the objects and moving them around. These are a very small Buddha figure, a white seagull feather, bark pieces from a sycamore tree, small rocks etched with animal images, various gemstones, and a blue blown glass heart from my granddaughter. Sometimes I play the music of Tibetan bowls during these meditations. It brings me peace.

# CHAPTER SIX

## Secret Societies

In old Europe, the enlightened ones, those who know, those who understand, banded together to preserve ancient wisdoms. Perhaps the secret societies emerged to keep the body of the esoteric intact, and to carry it forward for future generations.

The Magi (the three wise men from Persia) are one example. But we have had other elitist sects of scholars who have kept occult (meaning hidden) accounts of their findings alive.

The mystery school I am most familiar with is the White Brotherhood, into which I was introduced by my earliest teacher, Bertha Eaton. Some other secret societies of that era are the Golden Dawn, the Builders of the Adytum, and Dion Fortune's Society of the Inner Light. Possibly the name most familiar to the reader may be Rosicrucians or "The Order of the Rosy Cross". Each such esoteric society would have a system of degrees through which the student would advance from one degree to the next.

My grandfather, as an example, was a 32nd degree Mason. The Free Mason lodge emerged from the "Guild of the Stone-Masons" of long ago and it has remained intact to this day.

In the 1800's in Europe there arose "Societies for Psychical Research"—for the study of the paranormal. So it is, that through the ages there has always been recourse for the serious student who was ready to do the hard work. Some societies focus on healing in the vision mind, or the magic of visualization, where the light worker astral-projects his/her subtle body to help the one in need. Some of these practices involve the ability to focus and a deep level of meditation. But the work is legitimate and is being practiced in our day by dedicated light workers for the greater good of humanity.

# Light Workers

To the neophyte (beginner) a few words:

Light workers come from all walks of life. You may pass them on the street, or see them at the market place. They are normal, everyday people. Most keep a low profile, preferring to go about their esoteric pursuits quietly. Theirs is a lifetime commitment to serve the greater good.

As I have mentioned, the West always looks to the East for inspiration. Eastern Esoterism gave America the disciplines she was lacking. India gave us the practice of yoga and an understanding of breathing techniques and of the chakra systems.

The serous student of the mysteries will at some point choose to make some lifestyle changes such as taking time for meditation, instigating a change in diet, or finding a teacher. The main thing after the experience of a spiritual awakening is to KEEP ON GROWING!

The Tibetans tell us "if you leave your teacher (to go your own way), then watch your mind". Our sequence of thought patterns has been compared to a team of run-away horses (meaning out of control). The Mongols—the great horsemen of Asia's plains—compare the force of one's breath to "riding the wind horse."

In the initial part of my own training, I felt compelled to distance myself from most of my friends in order to spend time with my teacher. The knower within yourself will tell you if you are suited to the heavy demands of the esoteric life. We each have what I call "our contract with the universe". In the 1970's I was being driven toward my search for the sacred with no idea where it would lead. For those with a family or a day job, finding time for serious study demands a huge commitment. But let me remind you that some folks earn college degrees with both a job and a family in tow! So study is possible!

# Circles

The ritual circles of the stone masons began many years ago, near various stone quarries across Europe. At that time the members of the Guild reached back in history to King Solomon's temple to find their symbol, the two interlocked triangles of Judaism. This symbol that represents the thought: "As above, so below" to the members of the early Masons' Guild expressed a belief in a Supreme Being. I should note that the Seal of Solomon is also referred to as the "Double Seal" in other orders or societies.

Ceremonies using circles are ancient in their origin. The circle is represented as the "serpent biting its tail" called the "Oroborus"

The Wicca, pagan folk of old Europe, recognized that dancing in a circle would raise what they called a "cone of power." Mostly their dances were held at the full moon, in a grove of Oak, Ash or Hawthorn trees. Yes, I have danced that round.

I have also participated with our Native Americans in drum circles. Ceremonial circles can bring people together, to sing, dance, chant and drum. The drum speaks of our commonality, or as the Native Americans would say: We are all related, "Mitakueoyasin".

So we see that circles are a universal symbol, beginning in ancient times, and carrying forward to many forms of ceremony existing into the present times. I want you to consider the possibility that the parents you were born to might not have been a purely random thing! (Take a moment.) I realize this is a radical departure. I want to suggest that your choice of parents has everything to do with the Karmic baggage you carry from the past, and also the assignment you chose in order to erase some of the poor choices of previous lifetimes.

Though these lifetimes may not be present in memory, I believe some of us are "Old Souls". A few may have glimpses of a prior existence. Someone may remember being among the "landed gentry" or hold a soul-memory of "dancing the round" out of doors under the full moon. In today's usage the word "Pagan" has come to mean anyone who does not believe exactly as you do.

My belief is that each of us have worn many faces, and that you and I chose our (this time) parents in order to clear up some unfinished business from a long-ago lifetime. That might account for all the kids who figure they must have been adopted because they feel like "aliens" within their family group!

Many of us have ancestors who came from the British Isles, which was a real melting pot for invaders over the conturies. The fierce Vikings sailed down from the north in their long boats. The Saxons marched inland from what is now Germany and slaughtered the Celtic farmers working in their fields. And the Normans invaded from what is now France, all of them "spilling their seed" so to

49

speak. So you see none of us are pure "this or that" as far as genealogy goes.

About the Celts (pronounced Kelts)—they were Pagan; so I will use them as an example. The Celtic people love this green earth. They saw a relationship between the movements of the moon, stars and the affairs of man. The Druids, often mentioned in fact and in folklore, were the Priests among the Celtic people. According to written accounts, those on the British Isles had a written language, perhaps from the Runic alphabet handed down from the Norse invaders. They also had an alphabet of the trees; a form of sign language based on the digits of the fingers. They loved music, accompanied by "fife and drum". Among their numbers would also be the wise-woman who healed with herbal remedies.

I was reminded of the Celtic drummers while on a retreat with a group of about sixty feminists of various ages in Wisconsin. We came together under the guidance of a Master Drummer. Such was the energy in that circle that we literally drummed for hours, to the point of exhaustion.

## The Seasons

Four seasonal time passages that you can replicate, solo or with a group, are as follows:

March 21st Spring: Start by facing east. Think of it as a place of new beginnings Visualize the Earth-mother giving birth to new vegetation and all her creatures as you drum.

June 21st Summer: Face south. Feel the living earth beneath your feet. Be conscious of the abundance of the season; visualize abundance in your life. Drum.

September 21st Fall: Face west. Be aware of nature's bounty and the harvest time. Offer a prayer of gratitude for the harvest. Drum.

December 21st Winter: Face north. The earth is now in her wintry rest; in repose. It is a good time to acknowledge the passing of the seasons as a metaphor for the passages in our own lives. Now, visualize Mother Earth as sleeping. Drum.

Note: Drumming can heal the heart and clear the mind. Remember, work within a circle demands that everyone within the group be focused and aware of the shifts of subtle energy.

When I was active in circle work, my circles were never open to children or to dabblers or the curious, who lack the focus to maintain the energy a circle can generate. The level of energy I speak of is "pure intent".

# Guide of Souls

According to Greek Mythology, Hermes Trismegistus, "The Thrice Born", was a guide of souls through the "Hinter Lands", the dark and dangerous spaces. His status was that of messenger between the Gods and man. The Emerald Tablets which set forth laws for the coming generations are attributed to Hermes. The most notable is, "As above—so below". Meaning that universal law decries there is a higher level that governs the lowly affairs of mankind.

The role of Hermes in the guise of Guide of Souls has been reenacted across the centuries by various occult groups, secret societies and mystery schools.

I understand that in today's ceremonies of the Masons, the candidate is both hooded and blind-folded prior to entering the circle; very similar to the practices brought over from old Europe. In Wiccan circles the role of summoner imitates the Guide of Souls, by not only leading each participant into the circle, but to also "vouchsafe" for their right to be there.

Once again, the circle serves as a safe-place for a carefully choreographed dance. As we step into the "circle" during a ceremony, we are in fact leaving the everyday state of consciousness and entering a Rarefied space where our protection is assured and we can co-exist in an in-between "magical" state with the watchers at the threshold.

"This is a place that is not a place. This is a time that is not a time": as is said.

I have danced the dance of the deer with Brant Secunda. Funny thing, as we danced the blue sky clouded over and it started to rain. This—following a prolonged drought. In my own version of the deer dance, I use deer antlers and hooves. One person holds the two hooves, one in each hand, advancing and retreating, to the chant:

"I come, I glance, I dance, I prance",

while another person holds the antlers above his head. He is standing at the edge of the circle and he represents the "Lord of the Dance," or the Dance Master" dating back to the time of the cave etchings of Lascaux in France.

Sacred circles through time have used dance to cross the threshold between the mundane and the sacred. When we dance, our feet touch the ground beneath us, anchoring us, in part, to the elements of earth.

Meanwhile, we spin—echoing the wind. We move about as do the animals. We reach upward to the sun or stars. As humans we act as a conduit between the earth and the higher realms where the angels dance. This is the dance of ecstasy!

The "Animal Dancers" who lived in caves and wore the skins of animals were not so primitive as we may suppose. They knew how to dance themselves into a state of ecstasy that could call forth the prey they needed in the next day's hunt. Sympathetic magic was a huge part of their lives and also the means of the survival of the tribe.

# America's First People

In the early pages of this book I made mention about the resemblance of some of the tribal people I saw in the Pacific Northwest to the tribal people of Russia. Very recently I ran across a story in the New York Times on this subject. Let me pass these findings on to you because they enforce and enlarge what has already been disclosed about the ice-age migrations: Scientists now report that the first migrations from Siberia occurred 15000 years ago. Two smaller migrations would follow before the ice-bridge would melt into the sea. The newcomers to the Americas would fan out to eventually cover Canada, North America, Central America and South America.

Canada's Eskimos inherit about half of their DNA from these migrations. Language sources can also be traced back to the Yenisi Valley in Siberia.

This update was very exciting to me for two reasons. First of all, I've made a study of the connection between the Siberian tribal people and their "cousins" in this hemisphere. Moreover, I've long had vivid dream-scapes of living in Siberia, possibly as a member of the Evenk, Samoyed or Yakut tribe. In these dreams I am riding on a "Sledge", pulled along by one lone reindeer. There is snow-cover and as the sledge skims along, it squeaks over the hardened snow. The night sky in these dreams is a deep indigo dotted with oversize stars. The air smells crisp and clean, fragranced by fir trees.

I wonder if this is a dream-scape from a past-life experience. Quoting from author/anthropologist Piers Vitebsky, 1979: "North America was probably peopled from Siberia, by hunters who crossed the Bering Sea when it was a land-bridge."

By chance, when we lived in the Olympic Peninsula in Washington, we happened to be in close proximity to an ancient migration pathway. There was a historic "find" there in 1977 that brought the scientists and "National Geographic" people running:

One late summer day "Manny" Manis set out to excavate a pond on a soggy section of his farm. In doing this, he came upon two eight foot tusks of an ancient mastodon which had been there for 14,000 years. In addition to the tusks, several hundred other bones and some teeth were found. It was determined by archeologists that the huge mastodon had been killed by spears and butchered on the spot by per-historic hunters—possibly the descendants of the migration tribes who crossed the Bering Ice Bridge 15,000 years ago!

Angel in Flight ©

# CHAPTER SEVEN

## <u>Giving Up Things</u>
## (And Gaining Everything!)

Twenty or so years ago my husband Frank and I moved to Ottawa Lake, Michigan. They call it a town, but actually it wasn't much more than an old rickety bar, surrounded by farmers' fields. I loved living in Ottawa Lake because I could gaze at the 360 degree panoramic view outside my bay window. All sorts of animals came to visit our property, including the large snapping turtle that lived in our drainage ditch. Foraging groups of deer passed through. A mother raccoon and her two cubs checked out a hole in our mulberry tree. A mated pair of broad-wing hawks perched on the electric wires, waiting for something edible to pass underneath, and the owls called by night.

I remember telling myself at the time, that living in the midst of all this wildlife would possibly be the happiest time of my life. And it was! When the universe offers you something beautiful, hold out both hands and say "thank you"!

A few years later we were living in an old farm house with a white barn and a stocked pond where herons liked to stop for lunch. With five acres, my dog Moonshadow was at the height of her glory living there.

And I was writing! This book was about the Tree of Life, titled "Up the Tree". People came to my classes and sat for Tarot readings. I held outdoor drum circles and people drove down from Detroit and Traverse City. When Frank put in a vegetable garden, I put in a patch of wildflowers. Foxes barked at night and bullfrogs croaked endlessly on sultry summer nights. (Bear with me here, this is leading somewhere!)

The lesson is—if you are doing what you love, your work, your life is full! Whenever I am doing my work, teaching or writing, I don't care about much else. I don't care about going out for a meal, a movie or anything else. I do some of my best writing in my PJ's. In other words, I never feel I am giving up things because everything I love is right at my fingertips; my books, the songbirds outside the window; to me—less is more!

When our inner light expands everything else falls into its proper place and that includes the ego-self. It's funny how much attention we Americans pay toward looking good, having a new car, all the right technology, or being seen in all the right places! Toward what end?

I have to question why our culture has more trouble than any other with things of Spirit. Are we staying busy every moment to avoid . . . ourselves? Our mortality?

I have written this book to express another viewpoint: We never die! We recycle! You and I have been here many times, perhaps choosing our parents, or even knowing the life-lessons that will hone our soul's growth.

When I let go of my strong attachment to my childhood religion, I never for a moment lost my faith! In fact, after forty years of study and practice, my faith has deepened and broadened. At the point when I turned to Eastern esoteric studies, a place where many embrace a belief of reincarnation, my faith in the goodness of a divine system remained firm.

Reincarnation was a radical shift of perspective back in the 60's and 70's. Paramahansa Yoga-Nanda and Chogyam Trungpa had each brought their respective Hindu and Tibetan philosophies to America. This had set up a whirlwind for discussion and debate among those who were searching through alternate systems of spirituality.

Some of the members of my immediate family were upset by my interest in other spiritual systems. Some friends would walk away, but for over forty years my goal has remained the same: to understand the worlds of Spirit, and how they might interface with our physical World of Matter! Let me assure you that your own personal journey is equally unique! It will be yours alone, dependent on your karma (deeds both good and deeds not so good) from the past as well as the choices you will make throughout this lifetime.

I have found that those we meet along the way—those who are "different" in their perspectives—may prove to be your most important allies simply because they have developed a measure of tolerance through their own personal experiences.

If you are looking for a teacher, consider a person who is well-grounded in their own body of study, but has no personal "ax to grind". No good teacher should over-charge! But it is pleasing if you might bring a few oranges, a bunch of flowers or a box of chocolates, if they push aside other payment. It shows you respect the teacher and the teachings.

Beware the "fake" who has no sure footing in his own "Discipline" or is without any field of study. Do not become indebted to someone who appears "glamorous", who has no actual experience with his or her craft; but who feels free to charge you for his or her time. Be discerning!

# What is our Assignment?

Our universe is vast; the possibilities endless. In the teachings of Kabbalah our Earth experience is considered just a "kindergarten", a beginning place. Here we learn what it is to be truly HUMAN. There are higher levels ahead as we come into awareness of our true Spiritual Nature. Whenever we read, study, pray, or follow meditation practice—that is the beginning.

Each planet in our solar system emanates its own energetic vibration, which is interacting with the energy of the other planets, and is also influential to our receptive human nature. As we develop and evolve in one area we then can climb to the next level.

Always interested in the Native American part of my own heritage, I began looking for a teacher. On a retreat with Native American Teachers and Story-tellers, I was very impressed with a young woman, the fourteenth medicine woman in her family. When she offered apprenticeships in "Shield-making" scores of woman, including myself jumped at the opportunity.

One Native teaching is that animals are our teachers, and how they "will allow" themselves to be seen by us.

Actually the animals should be dreamed by the shield-maker, but perhaps they will also appear to us "in person". One's Animal Totems—and you can have several—are parts of the person you are. Their energy will be YOUR energy, and the apprentice may have several encounters before they come to understand—"Oh yes, that is my Totem!" Then they will portray that animal on their hand-crafted shield.

When finished, my shield depicted three images: the Deer, the Owl and the Hawk; all of which came to me within only a few days, in what I consider through Magical ways. My finished shield also displayed deer hooves, and two (found) bird feathers; one hawk, the other an owl feather. My Medicine Shield was finished!

# Light Workers

Soon after I had apprenticed with the Shaman, and completed my own Medicine Shield, I knew there was something more I should do. The Shaman's work is to enter the Dark, to heal the bodies, minds and spirits of those who suffer. Unexpected circumstances would lead me to the next initiation—that of a Light Worker.

In the middle of the night a man was shot on a downtown street by someone we knew. A musician, he was sentenced to five years detention. During that time I became his mentor. I wrote to him regularly, and my husband and I gifted him with a piano, so he could build a choir among the other prisoners. To his credit, he completed his education during his incarceration.

In 1990, shortly before I began offering my Shaman Apprentice Program, I heard from a young Native American, who was what is called a "Lifer" in jail jargon. He told me he was taking the rap for a woman who had stabbed someone to death. I will call this young man, still in his twenties, "Dark Horse." He was diligent with his lessons, which I sent him free of charge. We corresponded for the next three years.

When I took on my next young apprentice, he told me the warden was giving him a "hard time" about his Medicine Bundle. As part of the Program, I would provide certain objects, in this case, a small feather. I approached the Warden and we exchanged letters. I stated that, as Shaman, I was his spiritual mentor, and that my apprentice had a right, under law, to practice his native beliefs. We went logger heads over his rights. A Light Worker must have both courage and persistence

My next assignment as a Light Worker was to mentor another prisoner. He had gone on-line and had picked up a girl much younger than himself. He too was ordered to serve time. When it came time for his release, the entire community, most especially his church, shunned him! Following his release, I approached him in a public place with a big bear hug. A Light Worker must be prepared to enter a dark place and heal the soul of those who suffer alone.

Let me mention, scores of others are doing Light Work. I will cite the courage of a woman I know.

Every evening she takes a basket of sandwiches and walks the streets of downtown Toledo (this was in the 1980's) passing out food. Homeless men depended on her. Sometimes she would take a man into her home, wash his feet and give him clean stockings. I know this because I once provided a package of socks.

A Light Worker will be there to encourage and uplift those without hope. Many who do their work go unrecognized, knowing they must reach out for the good of suffering humanity. What drives these people? Perhaps a Karmic Debt from a long-ago past lifetime? I have no answers.

Years ago, a friend suggested to me "Won't it be interesting that a person who expects their heaven to be peopled by all-white Christian republicans, will see when they got there that it is a mix of ethnicities and religions, and that any of the rest of it is completely useless!"

I often think about this! Perhaps in past earth visits we may have been a Mongol warrior, or a Tibetan monk, or a Sufi dancer. THE

SOUL KNOWS ITS OWN JOURNEY! We do not yet know what we shall become, so it is a good policy to keep a generous world view toward those who are different than ourselves.

# Dark vs Light

When we are seriously into our studies, one question often leads to the next. For example:

Q. "Are we only the replicas of our ancestors?" Certainly not! We come in as "free flying" agents, each with our specific bundle of flaws and miss-steps; all of which we must overcome for our soul's development. Our talents and proclivities may seem to be genetic, but our assignment—"what we actually came in to do"—has little to do with our parents.

There are accounts in many ancient religions about the "Dark Angels". Some refer to Lucifer as a Daemon (or guardian angel) and to Satan as a Fallen Angel. Since the Ancients also believed that man (ourselves) had fallen from a "State of Grace" does that mean that we were once Angels, ourselves?

If you and I were once angels in good standing—does it stand to reason that we can reclaim ourselves? I like to believe that we evolve with each lifetime, hopefully spiraling upward, eventually becoming "the Best that is in us." The Buddhist speak of Buddha Nature—becoming kinder and more conscious in our awareness. Since I have written this book—"Dancing with the Angels", I would like your feedback on the ways we can do this!

Owl Woman ℅ S. Johnson
6197 S. Winding Way
Swanton, Ohio 43558

# Karmic Patterns

People often ask me about the word "Karma", believing it has a negative connotation, but that is not the case at all. Karma is accumulative in Nature. The word Samsara refers to the illusions of life; such as living in a fools' paradise. A loss of self-control leads us to a next round of rebirths, where we might fall back into old patterns of behavior. But we have been given the power of choice, to live mindfully, to practice discrimination!

Karmic patterns can lead us into similar addictions, or over attachment to certain people, i.e. (clutching) or the hoarding of more than we need. Things! Until we begin to live in conscious awareness, it seems we are doomed to the same cravings; say for red haired women, or vintage wine, or for a Chrysler convertible. Clutching, or hoarding, or treating people and animals badly, can all lead to multiple rebirths. Suggestion: Take up the practice of meditation, so your Karmic patterns might become more clear to you.

# Dreams and Images

When you are in a period of rapid psychic development, sometimes you can go into an overload. This is exactly what happened to me with the strangest-of-all series of dreams. Those dreams occurred soon after a visit with a Medium who told me I had a Guide named John Belvedere. What the Medium didn't tell me was that John Belvedere existed in another dimension which I had named "Elphane" in a children's book I was writing. We were living in Sylvania Ohio at this time, across the road from Lourdes College where I was taking art classes. It was a busy time in my life, when I was running on overload

That first dream was set on the campus of Lourdes College. In my dream I noticed a very short, strangely dressed man as I sat in the auditorium for a concert. After the concert he followed me to my car in the parking lot and introduced himself as John Belvedere. This tiny man was dressed in an English waistcoat and knickers—an outfit straight out of the 1800's. I couldn't help but notice that he came only to my chin in size but there was also something dapper about him; perhaps a dash of confidence.

After this first encounter, John Belvedere continued to appear to me in a series of unworldly dreams. In one dream, I turned off the road into an unpaved driveway near one of Centennial Road's stone quarries. About three hundred feet from the road and out of sight was a charming old-world cottage, set within some trees and wildflower gardens. Everything was so colorful and bright as to appear unworldly. As I approached the cottage, John Belvedere opened the door and invited me inside, as though he expected me.

Once again I noticed he was only 45 inches tall, but that he carried an enormous sense of power. He immediately told me that I was to "Stay with him FOREVER" and that we had been together "when the world was new." He even introduced me to a miniature boy and girl; his children in that dream. He instructed me that I was now the Lady of the House, and that I was to care for the flowers, which lay in colorful abundance on the table.

Looking back, I believe this series of dreams were about the Faerie Folk who exist in another dimension. I also believe I was traveling on a Green Ray of Netzach, the Nature Kingdom on the Tree of Life. Some of my dreams were once again set in the college auditorium. In one, there was a "cat walk" where Grey Nuns walked high above, while I was seated with John Belvedere at my side, watching them parade.

# Recording Dreams

The shortest way into the workings of the subconscious mind is through your dreams. It is a "Pan's Labyrinth" in there, for anyone who wants to sharpen his intuition or psychic abilities. My routine is as follows:

1) Write down your dream as soon as possible.
2) Read the dream over, looking for "catch phrases" or parts that reflect your life—past—present or future.
3) Underline the "clues" in your dream journal; the ones which offer you insights.
4) Save your old dream journals. They are pure gold; the keys to your psychic. Dreams can inspire us and also encourage us!

"Follow, Follow
Follow, Follow
Follow, the Fellow
Who follows his dreams"
        . . . an old Scottish ballad.

Nursemaid angel

# CHAPTER EIGHT

## Guardians, Guides and Gate Keepers

Many things, other than dreams, brought me to clearer psychic awareness. I'm remembering a private one hour session with a renowned Trance Medium from New York. Before she went into trance, I asked her for information about my Guides. She told me of a Master Guide, an Egyptian, and spelled out his name. The other guide, she called him my gate keeper, was a Native American Brave. She told me I would feel his presence in the wild places in Nature. Which I do! Whenever I feel fearful, he lets me know he is there by the sound of sticks breaking or a knocking on the walls. A third entity, a woman from Guatemala (circa 1700's) is a healer. When I am laying on hands for someone in pain, she will be there. These helping spirits will stay with me throughout this lifetime. I am not unique! I am as earth bound as my readers are in our collective humanness. Each of us have Guardians, whether or not we choose to acknowledge them. I would be amiss if I did not pass on this information!

# Where is Heaven?

Some wise person once said: "Heaven is under our feet as well as over our heads." I would like to add that the Angels are always close at hand. One's idea of heaven will depend largely of the influence of one's core spirituality. But, I would also include the importance of landscapes. For example the Native of a South American rain forest might dream of that. For the Inuit of the circum polar far north—his dream-space, or final resting space will be an all white landscape of snow, polar bears, arctic foxes or snowy owls.

For those who grew up in the heartland of America (circa the 1900's) our landscapes were mostly farmer's fields, woodlots and small towns. Having grown up in the latter, myself, I can attest that most of us grew up believing in the same things as our parents. I loved it when Gloria Steinem said "Most of us (women) are living out the unlived lives of our mothers!"

I have found that to be true. The upside of small towns is knowing we are safe within the dominant scheme of things. The downside was most of us never questioned what we had been spoon-fed within our small, confined communities.

Until I was in my late teens I never questioned the status quo! We went to church where we listened to the same "bill of goods" which had been spoon-fed to our parents. This concept of small, safe world would break up like an eggshell when I began to delve into alternative (esoteric) studies, and it has sat on shifting sands ever since.

I began to question the randomness of suffering, disease and death when my younger brother received a massive head trauma at age nineteen. One which would leave him permanently disabled. At his bedside, I watched him struggling to awake from the coma during the four months he lay shackled in his "in-between" world.

It changed my illusion of the once safe world. This is when I began my search for the sacred.

I began studying various philosophies because I could see that "Religions" and "Spirituality" are not the same thing. Spirit exists within ourselves, independent from whatever one's family or other cultural influences hold forth. It became clear to me that most churches had become "Big Business" and also political voices in our society. And so it was that I began MY FORTY YEAR SEARCH FOR THE SACRED.

As Russian Anthropologist, Piers Vitebsky has said "The Spirit World contains the true causes of things that happen in the ordinary world." My first wake-up call was that there are multiple levels beyond our five-sense world. These are the spaces inhabited by Spirit Entities variably called Angels, Ancestors, the Mighty Watchers, the Divas, the Departed Kin, are according to the development of one's belief systems.

Many other societies do not follow the HEAVEN versus HELL mindset which most of us are indoctrinated with. Many people believe we have a Soul which will re-locate in other realms where we will continue to evolve. Many believe we free-travel to wander among the teachers of a higher order, i.e., the Angels.

Some of the most influential teachers of my lifetime believe we only visit this Earth-experience for a "span of days" before returning to the Higher Realms. A few of those I've met have expressed their own lifelong "Search for the Sacred", believing they are chosen by the spirits from other realms to teach and inspire others on this Earth-plane.

Some of these instructors call themselves Light Workers. After 9-11 I received two phone calls. The first was a Biologist in California, who said "We Light Workers are having a hard time (with the carnage)! Another call came soon after from a local minister, who essentially told me "We Light Workers are having a hard time". I feel they were correct.

Following the current world upheavals, we always enter a new period of Adjustment. This tells me that those who are in touch with the cycles of man's evolution are feeling the currant shift of the Earth's Passages. Who was it that said "These are the times that try men's souls"?

Looking back to thirty years ago, I can see how my years of Shamanic studies shaped the way I saw not only human affairs, but more especially how our society's impact has hurt the development of other, weaker, countries around the world. We have not always been the "good guys"!

Shamanism has been called the world's oldest religion, predating the pyramids, the Persian Empire and the conquests of Genghis Khan. Here we have ancient people with "just one foot out of the cave", who had an intimate relationship with the "spirits of things". This included not only humans like themselves, but animals, birds, waterfalls and trees. They saw Spirit everywhere.

As the human dimension continues to evolve (come into conscious awareness), we must see more clearly, listen more deeply, and become better conservators of our Earth. With all our technology our awareness we sadly appear to lag behind.

The Tree of Life, mentioned under Kabbalah, has a counterpart with the Shamans of Asia. Their cosmos is seen as consisting of three worlds; an upper world, a middle world and a lower world.

For the indigenous Tibetan people prior to Buddhism (526 B.C.), their religion was Earth based, called the Bön. The Bön world was Shamanic, with a belief in Spirits, Mediums and Oracles who could fore-tell the weather for farmers. They also believed in "Soul Flight" similar to the "out of body" experiences recorded in many other societies. Buddhism, coming on the heels of the Bön, as it does, accepts the belief that one's lifetime may be limited in years, but that we will return as "new people" in future incarnations.

Buddhist doctrines encourage us to live mindfully, showing kindness (metta) to all living beings. I dream of the time when the whole world would accept these behaviors. May it be thus!

Across Asia, both male and female Shamans make Soul Journeys, once again documented here in America as "out of body" experiences. Reincarnation here and abroad is about the belief that the souls of the deceased will return at a future date, with new identities. In fact some teachers expect that to occur within a short framework of 1 ½ to 2 ½ years. Tibetan astrologers are also very talented in determining the geographic area to which the departed will next return.

I have mentioned that my fore-bearers were of Celtic, German, and Native American heritage. But, strangely, in this current lifetime my dreams are most often about (the Shamanic) Mongols, Tibetans and Siberian tribal people. In each of these ethnic groups the Shamans dance and drum themselves into a state of ecstasy, where they enter into trance. Some Shamans report they can ride the wild Wind Horse, or a Reindeer into the upper worlds. Others say they "ride on their Drum" and the Drum transports them. Our American Eskimo Shamans (original descendants of the migratory Mongols) use the "Soul Journey", leaving the body to travel through the air (upper world) to retrieve their patient's Guardian Spirit. Our American tribal people regard the Eagle as "The one who flies closest to the Great Spirit" The Eagle is honored throughout the tribes as sacred.

In dreamwork, I always consider dreams about Eagles as being spiritual in meaning; and dreams about snakes to be about personal power. Those along the Pacific Northwest coast, such as the Makah tribe, revere the Whale, taking great care to only harvest only one and to utilize every morsel; leaving nothing on the beach for the scavengers.

We need to remember that every spiritual system has its Deities. In our own past lives we have possibly worn many ethnic faces, and danced and drummed around many tribal campfires. If we could trace our multiple lifetimes they might include lifetimes as warriors, healers, artists and dignitaries. The tribal people who inhabit our earth are strong and resilient. It is not so surprising that their beliefs in the animal guardians and totemic helpers would be so far-reaching as is the importance they place on dreams.

Praying Angel ©  O.W

# CHAPTER NINE

## As a Man Dreameth

I have mentioned that I come from a long line of dreamers. Let me say I have plenty of company in my fascination with the dreamworld. The aboriginal Australians are known as the "People of the Dream-time". They co-existed within their dreams and expressed them through their very original artwork.

For many years, within the Owl Clan, we had a Dream Society where members brought their dreams to class. But if one's dream is not written down and told, it will soon evaporate and be lost to time.

As we dream—so we become. Without the dream, an idea of what and who we can become, we founder. As a man dreams his world, he enables that dream to become reality. Right now, I am dreaming this book. The words come together and I write them down. So it is with our lives; we dream our lives as we want them to be. Then we enter that reality and live within that creation.

Show me a dreamer and I can see a budding Shaman.

# Angels All Around Us

We of the pervasive American mind-set do in no way have a monopoly in our belief in the existence of Angels.

A local journalist tells us, "All the people of the Torah also believed in Angels—from Abraham the father of the twelve tribes of Israel, extending to Jacob who wrestled with the Angel while ascending and descending the ladder, to John the Baptist, Jesus and Mohammed—they all believed in Angels."

Turning to polytheistic religions with their many gods and goddesses, they too have their Angels—the shining ones called "Devi". Every system has its deities. In our past lives we have possibly worn many ethnic faces, in many areas around the globe, as we lived out any number of roles.

Reach into your own soul memories, if you are so inclined. This could make for some exciting group discussions.

# A Definitive Biblical Account

Angels play an important role in Biblical accounts found in both the old and new testaments.

We have annunciation, where the angel Gabriel appears to a young Jewish woman—perhaps still a teenager with the news that she will bring forth a holy child.

A mere thirty three years later, we see a sorrowing mother, Mary, along with the other Mary at the empty seplecur at the end of the Sabbath as it began to dawn on the first day of the week. The stone has been rolled back and the attendant Angel informs the women "We know that you seek Jesus who was crucified. He is not here, for he is risen. Christ the Lord is risen from the dead". A rejoicing chorus of Angels may have joined in, asking "Oh death where is thy sting? Oh grave where is thy victory?"

From the earliest times, when the scriptures were being handed down by "word of mouth," or oral tradition, the Angelic hosts bent near the earth, to interact with the forlorn, to comfort the bereaved and lift up the fallen.

# A Recent Visitation

It was the final night of the British Olympics. I remember it well—August 11, 2012 was to be the night of the shooting stars, the weatherman on TV had said. So I had to remind myself, to be sure to look at the eastern horizon where the crescent moon and Jupiter would be hanging in the sky.

About 5:30 in the morning, barely light outside, I saw a very tall man—his presence filling the door-way—to the left side of my bed. He was draping vines over a window. The leaves were shaped like Philodendron; three boughs, garlands in all.

When I first saw him I let out a little "uh" in surprise. The figure wore a plaid shirt and work pants, what a regular florist might wear, and he looked at me as if he knew I could see him. I had the psychic impression that he had been a soldier in one of the wars. His chin and cheekbones were chiseled, and his expression was very calm. I was certain he meant me no harm, but that his being there brought a healing. The words "blessing-way" came to mind. This visitation was the most visible of all, but unlike the first one, it evoked no fear only peace.

# The Tibetan

There are many accounts of people on their death-beds, seeing family members waiting for them. Some accounts seem realistic to this listener. Why, when we are out-of-body and able to travel with the speed of thought, wouldn't we want to be at the bedside of the loved one who is ready to make transition?

At 5:10 AM on August 22nd, 2012 I had yet another visitation. In the pale per-dawn light an Entity stood just an arm's length from the right hand side of my bed. This visitor appeared to be Tibetan, or perhaps Mongolian or of a Bhutan ethnicity. He was dressed in a dark silk robe with an intricate design and his hair was pulled back into a single braid. His hands folded at waist height and he bent slightly toward me with a calm, intense gaze.

I sprang instantly awake, THEN QUICKLY REALIZED I WAS NO LONGER AFRAID! These angelic visitations had become common place for want of a better word. I believe the entities are all around us, but we have become hardened during our many visits to an insensitive world, and have mostly lost our ability to discern their presence.

# A Village Shaman

A while back I had a Muslim lady-friend. She was a doctor from Kashmir which is on the boarder of India. She told me that everyone from her section of the world has their astrology chart done—beginning with the day of their conception.

My friend also put me in touch with a professor friend of hers' back in Mumbai, who was known for his skill in erecting astrology charts. We began to correspond, and it seemed the professor and I shared a fondness for the English poet William Wordsworth. As time passed, he did send me a copy of my Natal (birth) chart.

77

As I remember, it was square in shape, and meticulously drawn out by hand.

As I traced back the months before my birth, it appeared that I was conceived under the sign of Libra, "the Scales". Natives of Libra have some qualities I've always admired in others. Librans are known for being fair and generous people, always pleasant to have around.

My doctor friend also told me something about her "Village Shaman", back home. She said he lived in a small house at the edge of a cemetery. Every morning the local villagers would line up, parking themselves in the shade of the tombstones, until he was ready to see his first patient. There would be a steady line of people stretching through the heat of the day. This Healer was a powerful draw for the helping spirits from the other side. She said that when the Shaman was "curing" the floors and the walls of his house would shake, so strong were his powers. Most importantly the Shaman never charged his patients a fee.

My friend was a fount of eastern folklore, which she was quite willing to share. For example, she told me that if I would stand under a "certain tree" at the "full of the moon" an Angel would come to me. She also shared the name of her personal Guardian Angel. Of course I believed her! Why would I not? I've been dancing with the spirits for many years myself.

Often a holy man—a Saddhi—will go on a retreat, alone on a mountainside or some other wild place. There he will live in seclusion, in contemplation for many years. Food is left outside his door by devotees (followers) but he will remain in silence, never speaking during his stay. The villagers look to the Holy Man as their inspiration. I mention this as an example, to compare it with my own, very brief, attempt at silence.

Yes, there are cultural differences. We are not taught early in childhood to focus, or to sit quietly as a discipline. Americans are into acquisition, wealth and prosperity as their priorities, rather than love of learning for its own sake. Few of us take any time out for personal spiritual practice.

# <u>Silence</u>

"Too soon old. Too late wise." . . . . anon.

During the middle ages everyone across Europe was searching for the Philosopher's Stone, which would turn lead into gold. Today, we hope for the winning lottery ticket. We still cling to the false assumption that happiness lies somewhere outside ourselves. We crave excitement, newness, lots of hoopla—even though the fast pace wears us down and gives us ulcers.

Last April I told my friends I would make an honest effort, for just one week, to live in silence. My husband would be on the west coast, so I could shape my days any which way I chose. Perhaps I would work on this manuscript. Or, I could just give my mind and my mouth a rest.

The Buddhists call that mind-chatter we can't seem to turn off "Monkey Mind". When you live in a society like ours, where the goal is to stay busy and fill every moment with chit-chat, it's hard to turn it off! Once alone, all I wanted to do was "Embrace the Silence". First thing was to take the phone off the hook, and turn off the TV. I'd already stocked up with easy to prepare meals. Time to just settle in.

April is always my favorite month of the year. At dusk you can hear the Green Tree Frogs singing in their high-pitched voices down in the ditches. The colorful warblers are migrating through Ohio and the yellow daffodils out in the bulb garden are in full bloom. All around me lady spring is in the various stages of her rebirth. With this feast for the eyes and ears not for one moment did I feel alone.

Each day was magical. Mornings I meditated and offered up my gratitudes. Any dreams of merit were recorded in my dream journal. I caught up with my mail, and walked the letters to North Carolina, Seattle, or Florida down to the mailbox. The sweet smell of springtime was everywhere. I'd stand a while in the flower beds, just to let the warming sun brush off the winter blahs. The sights, sounds and smells of spring are enough to fill even the coldest hearts with gratitude.

At the time we are wrapped up into the political bickering, the war news or the accounts of crime on our city streets, we may not even notice what an impact it is having on our feelings of well-being. It robs us of our joy, and takes away our ability to live in the now, the moment! Without the TV news to bring me down, or those pesky telephone solicitations to interrupt my work, I could feel a new lightness in my house's vibration. Surely Angels were about.

I drifted through these quiet days with a sense of serenity—thankful for the sudden rain shower, the new buds emerging on the trees, the soft dusk, the radiant dawn all wrapped up together. One day I realized I was no longer dwelling on the past or worrying about the future. I was fully living in each moment as it presented itself.

Now, I realize not everyone has as much free time as the very young, the retired, or the elderly. But there's a lesson here! Each of us has to make our own spiritual retreat. Time spent alone and in silence refreshes the mind and nourishes the soul.

# Guardian Angels

It has been said that the more we learn, the less we realize we actually know. I continue to be perplexed about the difficult start in life so many children will receive. It is believed we all start our lives "in neutral" but the playing field is never even. Environmental and parenting skills play such a huge role in how we develop. In a perfect world each baby would be hoped for and cherished. But we know this is not the case. My opinion is that not everyone should attempt to parent, because some may not have the temperament nor the patience parenting demands. Without their basic creature needs met, some babies will fail to thrive.

There is a history of esoteric accounts about the Angels at the crib-side who keep watch. Blessed is the newborn who will be nurtured and guided through his childhood years by a pair of enlightened parents.

Our personal Guardian Angels come into our lives on the day we are born, and will stay with us until we depart this lifetime. We are told these guardians can most strongly be felt when we are about to stub our toe or fall off our tricycle. As we age, we may turn our backs on these invisible helpers, because we are impatient to get on with our independent lives. (My guess is at about the age of twelve or thirteen!) However, those who are more sensitive in nature may continue to be aware of the vibrational shifts as the Angels are passing through.

This seems to correlate with the image of "the Watcher at the crib-side". My belief is that those guardians who are assigned to small children will ease them out of their "human shells" in times of peril. There are many recorded cases of near-death experiences where children hold a vivid memory of the kindly figure who brought them to safety.

# CHAPTER TEN

## <u>Rising on the Planes</u>

This is what my Kabbalist teacher called the levels that exist just beyond the Earth level. These higher levels are said to be "peopled" with orders of Angels, Devas, and all manner of spirit helpers who watch over our earthly "goings on". Even though I was eager to make contact with these Advanced Beings, no one I met could give me a formula. Somehow I envisioned that the planes might have something to do with an index of colors!

The seven primary colors of the chakra system gave me my first clue—with each color having its correlating emotion. Possibly, I reasoned, those on the other side existed in color frequency or a tonal vibration (such as with Tibetan Bowls)! So sound and color could both be keys.

During my meditations, as I lay on my back with eyes closed, it was never DARK! In fact various color tones would "wash across" my (3rd eye) inner vision, similar to watching a small TV screen.

I turned to Kabbalah, using the colors of the ten Sepheroth on the Tree of Life (except for black or gray) as my references. In my meditations I never see murky, or dark colors—all are bright and distinct—including the pastel shades.

Could each of the people around us have a principle color they relate to? Does ENERGY itself have a color? These are questions that arise.

For instance, if I "tuned into" a gardener, someone who loves this green earth—would I contact her by calling the Green-Ray? Or, remembering my Mother, who always identified herself with the color orchid, while her twin sister drove a blue car and always furnished her house in shades of blue, would I call the Orchid or Blue-Rays? Even though they stayed in close affinity throughout their lives, there were vibrational differences. Or, how about an "artsy" person, someone into the theater or performance art. Would they respond to the color orange? While a psychic or visionary might operate on the indigo blue of their third eye. Of course I'm still speculating on the possibilities

Usually I begin my meditations with red, at the root chakra, and work my way upward to an intense violet. This is the color where I feel I can best reach the Helpers, Guides and Guardians. Through the years this is the system I've developed for "Rising on the Planes".

First, enter a deep state of meditation. (I find the practice of meditation is essential to all work involving the Higher Levels!) Start out with 5 minutes a day.

See which colors arise of their own free accord. Then, just allow the colors to flow across the screen behind your forehead. With practice you will be able to see the colors as they come in and they fade. If you are without a personal teacher's guidance, do some study of the seven Chakra colors and also learn to identify the colors of the energy centers (Sepheroth) on the Tree of Life.

I believe we each are wired differently and therefore vibrate at our personal color frequency. Other factors are your state of development and your desire to learn. Always remember to pursue the gifts you are being given for the good of humanity.

Some psychics are able to "read" people by the colors in their aura. These rainbow hues will vary from time to time according to one's state of health or emotional state. We study, we learn, and we develop our potential gifts. Everything, be it a flower, a stone or a tree, emits its own specific energy. Each of us is a composite of particals of energy. Like snow-flakes, each of us is unique.

# It's Your Path

For those who are ready to embark on your own "Search for the Sacred", perhaps these guidelines for observing color-rays, or deep listening to musical tones, or detecting fragrances, or receiving psychic impressions as they arise will help in your further development on the path.

You will know you are developing your heart Chakra when feelings of compassion arise. Look for deeper eye contact in another's eyes. Many others are lonely or dealing with loss in their lives. Strive toward feelings of accord or commonality.

Many times I have sought out the person who is different; the one of another ethnicity or belief system; and as many times I have learned from those encounters. Look for a glimmer of humanity in another's eyes!

Why do I search for meaning in the faces of those whose lives have been different from my own? Because the better we understand their teachings and their Pathways, the better we will understand the complexities of our own lives.

Our Native Americans have much to teach us. We also have much to gain from those teachers from the Near East; from India, Tibet, Mongolia, and extending north toward the tribal Siberians.

By seeing into their worlds we learn we are not so very different. We are one human family! We all wear our similar "Human overcoats" which cover our Tender Hearts and Bright Spirits underneath. We each carry with us our many lifetimes of human experience.

Namaste'

# Epilog

When I first began to comprehend the availability of the hosts of Angelic Beings around us, it was overwhelming. I hesitated whether or not to put some of my experiences into print.

"Perhaps the readers will see my book as just another piece of outer-space fiction", my careful and introverted self was saying.

But another part of myself was stronger, telling me to be honest in presenting each experience; to give it my best efforts and to speak from the heart. And this is what I have done.

Owl Woman